Hammer-Proof

A Positive Guide to Values-Based Leadership

Hammer-Proof

A Positive Guide to Values-Based Leadership

by

Jeffrey A. Zink, Ph.D.

Peak Press
Colorado Springs

Printed by Gowdy Printcraft Press, Inc.

Printed in the United States of America.

ISBN 1-892360-00-4

First Printing, May, 1998

For my father,
the finest example of integrity
I will ever know.
Chief, you're with me always.

Acknowledgements

Acknowledging the help you've received on a monumental task is a lot harder than it looks, at least if you want to keep it to a few paragraphs. I know that in the case of this book, I could never have gotten to this stage without the love, encouragement, and well-timed guilt of a lot of people.

So, at the risk of offending some whom I love, I'll keep this very short. My dear and trusted friends, Jeff Rhodes and Harold and Debbie Howell, gave willingly of their time, poring over this manuscript and making brilliant suggestions for improvement. Their meticulous and thoughtful care has made this a much better book than it started out to be. Similarly, I am deeply grateful to Charlie Eitel for taking time from his globe-trotting schedule to read it from a senior corporate executive's viewpoint.

There is no doubt that this book would not exist without the constant prodding (trust me, that is no exaggeration) of my awesome big brother, Dr. J. Zink, who blazed this trail before I arrived. I owe him a debt of gratitude that will be hard to repay; this book is merely a first installment.

If this book wouldn't exist without J., I wouldn't be who I am without my wife and best friend, Diane, who put her own personal development on hold many times in my twenty-year military career, and helped this effort along with her very special brand of prodding.

Lastly, I thank my two boys, Aaron and Trevor, who, as they mature toward manhood, continue to provide me with daily inspiration for life. God has blessed me with two of the finest, most loving human beings he has yet to create. For that I am deeply grateful.

Introduction
By
J. Zink, Ph.D.

My brother has written a tidy little smash of a handbook for ethical survival. Called *Hammer-Proof*, it certainly is that. And more. The ground it breaks is that unlike most philosophical treatises which we have all no doubt suffered through. The book reads easily, makes delightful sense, and is an eminently digestible psychoactive medication for a world gone ethically mad on most days.

But the real story here is my brother. Jeffrey is a real live American hero. A bombardier who has flown more than 2,000 hours in the belly of the great beast B-52, Jeffrey received in 1981 the first Air Force Air Medal given to a bomber crew since the Vietnam era for his role in leading the navigation of six B-52's flying non-stop from Grand Forks, North Dakota, to Cairo, Egypt, during Operation BRIGHT STAR. The bombers arrived on target within one-half of one second of the time they said they would be there. Next time you are late for church by a few minutes, think of six monsters flying 31 hours, doing 5 mid-air refuelings, and Jeffrey never even looking out the window (the navigators have no windows in B-52s).

This book of his is a window. Through it, you can see your own soul.

Often the superheroes we meet in life are people who sacrifice their families for their owns "careers." This is not Jeff. He is my hero because he loves his wife, Diane, and his children, Aaron and Trevor, and backs up that love with his presence, patience, and participation in their everyday lives. Jeffrey is a man who has walked in the path of the Lord his entire life; I am proud to be his brother. After you read the simple wisdom of his wonderful words, you will see how lucky I have been to be there throughout the years and watch this remarkable person discover his enlightened path.

Jeffrey is the master if you wish to learn the art of becoming hammer-proof. Leadership is the art of the ethical. This book nails it.

CONTENTS

Forward

I want to tell you something right up front: This book is written by a philosopher.

But please don't put it down just yet. It is written by a philosopher, but it's as far removed from standard philosophy as I could possibly make it.

Let me make a confession to you: To this day, I still have no clear idea why I decided to study philosophy. I certainly never intended to use it for anything productive! I do remember my first experience in a philosophy class. It was during the fall semester of my freshman year at the University of Virginia in Charlottesville. I took an introduction to logic class, and had a great time with it. The precision, the structure of logic, struck a chord deep within me. So in the spring I decided to take a symbolic logic class, and the chord sounded even louder. One homework set and I was hooked.

Since I was sure I was going to law school after graduation, and since the U.Va. Law School admissions office told me they didn't really care what their applicants majored in, I decided to stay with Philosophy. I'm sure YOU have made many life decisions for much more solid reasons.

In any case, I soon found out that philosophers—real philosophers, not the sort of wannabe mathematicians who wrote logic books—didn't spend a whole lot of time in the crisp, black-and-white world of deductive proofs. And their writing showed it. I found the works of philosophers—classical to modern—to be generally tedious and very difficult to understand. "Is that what makes this writer great?" I would ask myself. "Why can't he (invariably, the philosophers were men) just get to the point? If he has something important to say that will have an effect on people's lives, why does he insist on hiding it?" It was like some sinister Easter egg hunt where the object was to frustrate the hell out of anyone foolish enough to play.

Twenty-four years of reading philosophy has only confirmed my initial opinion. Anything that begins to approach the level of ordinary human understanding is panned as not scholarly enough. Now I can almost understand trying to keep the riff-raff out when discussing metaphysics, or epistemology or some obscure concept in ontology. (Come to think of it, keeping out the riff-raff shouldn't be that tough—who in their right mind would even want in?) But what really puzzles me is that this intellectual elitism extends to the study of ethics.

Ethics—the examination of how we ought to treat our fellow human beings and the world around us. Ethics, of all things, should be easily accessible to everyone. If you have a better way to live in peace and harmony, respecting the fundamental worth of other beings on this planet, why would you bury it in the confusing language of academia? To hide away the discovered truth about ethics would be like the automobile industry hiding away the secret of a car that can run more efficiently and without the pollution of an internal combustion engine. Or the cigarette industry hiding research which shows that nicotine is addictive and smoking can kill you. Or like...

Oh.

Never mind.

Now I'm not claiming that I have the answer to a better world. But if there is even a remote chance that what I have to say may help someone be a better co-worker, a better manager, a better CEO, a better parent or spouse, I surely don't want to lose that opportunity in an effort to show you that I own a thesaurus.

My goal in writing this book is to show you that you can make a difference, a real, positive difference in the lives of those you touch every day. What I have to share with you is not rocket science (or metaphysics, for that matter). It's pretty simple stuff, actually. A few basic tools to help you navigate the ethical "choke points" that crop up too frequently in our professional and personal lives.

Starting Points

Karen was attractive, intelligent, and successful, having risen to the senior rank of lieutenant colonel in the United States Air Force. Not a bad achievement in what is still a male-dominated environment. In fact, she was less than a year away from her first career milestone of 20 years. But she wasn't thinking about leaving the Air Force just yet. Too many things to do; too many goals to meet. She just wasn't done. She had two children of whom she was very proud, and was doing a more than passing job of balancing career and parenthood.

The only cloud on Karen's horizon was her marriage. As with many couples after years of marriage, theirs was not the romance it started out to be. What they needed was time—time apart, time to sort out their feelings and decide what was next.

The Air Force conveniently provided that time. Karen received a new assignment to another location across the country. Her husband was well established in his job, so here was the right opportunity to gain some distance and perspective. The kids were happy in school, so she decided to move on her own to the new assignment.

For a year or so, things progressed slowly. The kids were OK, but her marriage didn't seem to be improving much. It was then that she made the mistake. A small mistake. Understandable. She met someone else, someone who seemed to give her exactly what she had been missing all these years. And she began to fall in love. She didn't plan it; it just happened. This would obviously put a new strain on her marital problems, and she and her husband would have to work through it, like so many couples every day. But in Karen's case, there was a different and troubling twist to the story. Her new-found lover had chevrons on his sleeve—he was a sergeant in the Air Force. Military rules and regulations prohibit any personal relationships between officers and enlisted persons, even if there is no formal supervisory function between them. The uniquely military crime of fraternization is punishable under the Uniform Code of Military Justice. And so is adultery.

When he found out, Karen's commander brought the full force of military law down on her, even though the affair had been over for eight months. The court martial he convened found her guilty and sentenced her to dismissal and loss of all pay and benefits. Faced with the dismal prospect of finding private health care for her chronically ill daughters, Karen went to her parents' home, waited until they left for church, took her dad's shotgun out of the closet, pointed the gun at her head and pulled the trigger.

✧　　✧　　✧

July 17, 1981 was a typically hot and muggy Friday night in Kansas City. A young woman named Betty Nelson went with her friends to a tea dance—sort of a throwback to the 1940's, with a big band playing swing music of the era. She was joined by 1500 other dancers at a spectacular new hotel in downtown Kansas City, the Hyatt Regency, which had been open for about a year. And it really was breathtaking! Walking in the front door, you entered a massive, five-story atrium of glass and steel, connecting the two main towers of the hotel. The most prominent features in the atrium were the three walkways—sky-bridges linking the towers. There were bridges at the second, third and fourth floors, with the fourth directly above the second and the third offset from the other two by about 15 feet.

The place was really hopping by 7:01 as the band started into Duke Ellington's "Satin Doll," with the main floor crowded and dancers swaying to the music on all the skybridges. Just then a small cracking noise could be heard; it was followed by a noise like thunder that cut through the music. As the dancers turned toward the sound they saw a horrifying, surreal sight. The fourth floor bridge began to fall as the nuts securing the support rods to the structural box beams gave way. That bridge, with 50 or so people on it, dropped down onto the second floor bridge, crushing the 100 people on that walkway, and sending both bridges two more floors down onto the crowded dance floor below.

In fifteen seconds it was all over, except for the efforts of the rescue workers who removed the bodies of 114 victims and 200 more who were seriously injured. Betty found herself trapped in a pile of concrete and twisted metal. But she was alive. An older woman lying on top of Betty's ankles was not so lucky. As she waited for rescue, Betty could here the woman alternately scream and groan in agony. Then she got very quiet, and Betty knew she was dead.

Almost as soon as the rescue efforts got underway, the questions began. How could something like this happen? It took over 3½ years to get all the answers, and even today some conclusions are in dispute.

The original plans called for a continuous rod to run from the second floor through the fourth and then be attached to the steel girders in the roof. However, someone in the fabricating company (Havens Steel) decided that it would be too expensive to have to thread that entire rod, so they redesigned the support to use two rods, one attached to the ceiling and the fourth floor, the other (offset by about 4 inches) using the fourth floor to support the second, which in effect doubled the load on the connecting nuts.

The fabricators made the plan changes and called the engineering firm, GCE, to get the approval (a phone call that GCE denies ever getting). Havens also sent the revised plan, along with a package of 42 other changes, back to GCE for their stamp of approval, which they got. The contractor then built the atrium to the revised specs, and the rest is history.

In the immediate aftermath of the tragedy, Missouri Governor Kit Bond declared, "We do not know the cause of this tragedy, but we do know that the structural integrity and safety of the building had been assured by the architects, the contractor and in subsequent building inspections."

Somewhere, the assurance was flawed.

✧   ✧   ✧

Why start a book about a *positive* guide to values-based leadership with these obviously depressing stories? First of all, because values-based thinking has a real effect on our everyday lives, sometimes in dramatic and terrifying ways. Bad thinking about ethics chips away at our character, our very soul. On the other hand, good thinking about ethics can help us make the best choices for ourselves and the people around us.

But there's a bigger reason. I have spent the better part of the last 15 years studying stories like these and many others. The one common element in the most tragic of these stories is that they are not about common criminals who deserve to be locked away. No. These are stories about ordinary people, like you and me, people who believed with all their heart that their ethics were OK. "If I thought it was wrong, I wouldn't have done it. I just didn't think what I was doing was all that bad." Now we could sit back and shake our heads at them indignantly and deny their claim. Maybe some of them are just making things up. But most are being honest.

Their honesty shows us something about them, and about us. They aren't—and we aren't—bad people. We're basically good people who sometimes make bad ethical choices.

Often we make bad choices because we suffer from a disease, a disease which *Wall Street Journal* columnist

Vermont Royster called, back in 1975, "moral myopia," a short-sightedness that leads people to do things without seeing the ethical big picture in which they are acting. People like Karen and the Hyatt engineers aren't consciously bad. The real problem is they're not *consciously* anything—they're often simply not thinking about what they're doing. Unfortunately, in ethics as in law, ignorance is no excuse.

So what can we do about cases like these? Well, it seems we have two choices: We can look down our righteous noses at these poor suckers who got caught. Or we can examine what we and those around us can learn from these incidents. I think you'll agree that the second choice is a better choice.

That's what this book is all about.

It's straight talk about simple concepts that can make a difference to you and your co-workers, beginning today. It's practical advice about how to be a better leader, regardless of your salary or title or parking spot.

You know, if you think about it, there are only three kinds of events in life: red lights, green lights and yellow lights. Red lights and green lights are easy; you stop or you go. But what do you do when you hit a yellow light? (Yes, I know, if you're like most of us, you accelerate.) What about an *ethical* yellow light, where the decision is anything but easy? And as you know, the higher your position of responsibility, the more often those yellow light events land on your desk. Anybody can handle the red and green ones; not so with the yellows. The tools I have to offer I hope will make you a better yellow light navigator.

And if you get lost or confused along the way, just put the book away, because that means I will have failed to keep my part of the bargain.

But I'm betting you won't get lost.

So let's get on with it.

Who Cares About Ethics?

Well, at least I'd like to get on with it. But before we can make this journey together, I have to get over one large hurdle—the crossed arms. It's an attitude I see at least once in every audience I address.

"You're going to teach me about ethics? Yeah, right. I'm just here because I have to be, and you, with your fancy Ph.D., don't know anything about what life is really like in my job. I have a boss [or a set of stockholders or a community of citizens] who doesn't give a flip about ethics. All they care about is me getting the job done. Did I meet my numbers? Did I carry out my mission? Did the bottom line look good? That's all. And since that's who's paying the bill—writing my paycheck— that's all I care about, too."

Some version of that monologue may be running through your head at this point. Maybe you're thinking that ethics is irrelevant, or worse, that baseball manager Leo

Durocher was right, nice guys do finish last. Or maybe you buy into the "dirty hands" view of business (borrowed from the world of foreign affairs): "Of course I'm a good spouse or parent, I obey the law, pay my taxes, even go to church regularly. But it's a dog-eat-dog world out there in my business, and I sure don't want to come to the office in Milk-Bone underwear. Ethics is OK at home, but at work I have no choice but to get my hands dirty."

Maybe you're not quite that blunt, but let's face it: No matter where you are in your career, you have gotten— like the rest of us—very adept at separating the information you receive into two piles: The stuff that helps you get your job done, and the stuff that gets in the way. Because the bottom line drives the train, you want to drive faster, farther, and you certainly want to dump off anything that slows you down.

This won't be much of a surprise, but I think ethics belongs in that first pile. Ethics and values-based thinking will help you get your job done, *no matter what your job is.*

But it won't unless you believe it, too.

You are the only one who can make a difference—a real, positive difference—in getting that job done ethically. You are the key, the "point guard," in making that happen. I can write until my fingers fall off, with no effect. You, however, need only buy into these simple concepts, and it will start paying off.

But first I have to convince you that it will make a difference. So let's see what we can do.

A Case Study:
Leadership at Its Worst

One of my objectives in writing this book is to keep the mood light and upbeat. So far (given the stories I told you in the first chapter), I haven't done so well! It will get better. I promise.

But before it does, it's going to get worse. I promise you that, too.

I want to tell you a story about what happens when leaders forget their moral obligations to those they lead, to those they serve. It's a story that is as depressing as it gets.

You know, in story-telling school, they teach you never to tell the ending of the story first. But I'm going to break that rule, and tell you the end of this one.

It ends with four young widows. It ends with a bunch of fatherless children. It ends with four dead aviators, officers in the United States Air Force. It also ends with one destroyed B-52 bomber at Fairchild Air Force Base, near Spokane, Washington, on June 24, 1994.

I'm going to tell you this story not only because it's a classic bad example of values-based leadership, but because I knew personally and admired all four of those flyers; three of them I counted among my friends. It's a very painful story to tell, but it needs to be told, so maybe their deaths won't be a complete waste.

Let me tell you about each of the crewmembers aboard that airplane. First was the pilot in charge of the flight, Lieutenant Colonel Arthur "Bud" Holland. Bud was the premier Evaluation Pilot at Fairchild, responsible for setting and enforcing flying and safety standards for all other pilots assigned to fly B-52's. He had logged over 5,000 hours of flying time during his 23 years as a pilot, and had developed a reputation as an outstanding pilot, maybe the best B-52 pilot in the Air Force. He could make that lumbering hulk of an airplane do things you just wouldn't believe.

In fact, he was so good that people at Fairchild would call him "Mr. Airshow." Whenever the base had a special event or flying demonstration, Bud would get the call, because he could always thrill the crowds.

Bud knew the flying regulations inside and out, but beginning in 1991 he began to do things outside those limits. We all knew he pushed things pretty far, but we all believed it would be OK—he could handle it.

I remember very well the only time we flew together, in the winter of 1990. Bud had an aura about him that set him apart. Aloof, really. I was a Major at the time, a bombardier (also known as a radar navigator), and had been at Fairchild about six months. Bud was a Lieutenant Colonel, so we were pretty close in rank. But I remember riding out to the airplane on the aircrew bus, glancing over at him sitting across the aisle and thinking, "Wow, it's really Bud Holland. I'm going to get to fly with him." I was awed, as were many people.

We were scheduled for a fairly typical B-52 flight that night. About 9½ hours, during which we would fly about 3 hours at low level to practice evading enemy radar. To do this, we would fly between 250 and 400 feet off the ground at about 450 miles per hour through the rugged terrain of the Rocky Mountains in Wyoming, Idaho, Utah, Colorado and South Dakota. During the day, this was sporting. At night, it could be downright terrifying.

As the bombardier, I had one job during the low-level flight, until we got to the bomb run: Keep us from hitting the ground. Mountains do not take kindly to B-52's; the airplane invariably loses the confrontation. The way I kept us from hitting a mountain was to watch the terrain on my radar scope very carefully. I could see when mountains were looming up ahead of us, getting closer at the rate of about one mile every eight seconds. And I could tell when we were on a collision course. Since I didn't have any flight controls myself, I got very skilled at saying one word to the pilot. The word was, "Climb." Oh, sometimes I'd throw in a variation or two. "Climb, Pilot." Or "Climb, damn it." But usually it was just "Climb."

I had one other instrument to help me keep the crew alive—a 12-inch closed-circuit TV monitor for a camera mounted in the front of the airplane. In addition to giving

me a view of the outside world (navigators in B-52's
don't have a window—they ride in the "basement"), the
monitor also displayed the radar altimeter reading in the
form of a white strip that told me how high off the ground
we were.   It was set so that it blinked annoyingly
whenever we flew too low.

Throughout the flight that night, I spent a lot of time
telling Bud to climb, and watched that white strip blinking
at me, as if to say, "You're going to die. You're going to
die."   And all night long I carried out a little mental
dialogue with that ribbon. "No, I'm not. No, I'm not.
It's Bud Holland up there. He's the best. He won't kill
me."

I came through the flight unscathed, but I certainly
understood the reports I heard later that Bud had begun to
develop a pattern of violating the rules and regulations of
flying safety. Documented examples appeared regularly
over the next two years.   Fellow crewmembers at
Fairchild complained about his flying.   Some flatly
refused to fly with him, at the risk of violating a military
order. Bud's incidents were well known, yet the few

verbal reprimands he received from his commanders were
ineffective.

Let's talk about the second flier in the airplane that day,
sitting in the jump seat between the two pilots. He was
Colonel Robert Wolff, the Vice Wing Commander of the
Bomb Wing. I knew him simply as Bob. You see, I met
Bob 15 years earlier when I was a young lieutenant
navigator at Grand Forks Air Force Base, North Dakota.
Bob was a major and was my Flight Commander. He is
and will always remain one of the people I look up to in
my life.

I can remember clearly standing in Bob and Nan Wolff's
kitchen during a party, having a beer, when I mentioned
to him that the Air Force Academy had contacted me
about teaching philosophy. (I only had a bachelor's
degree at the time.) I was unsure about what to do—in
fact at the time I really didn't even know where the
Academy was located! But Bob had just come from the
faculty and told me, in his beautiful Texas drawl, what a
great place it was. I recall after that how he and Nan took
my wife and me under their wing, and treated us as peers,
despite the fact that I was very much his junior—and

merely a navigator! I took his advice about teaching at the Academy, and that, as Robert Frost put it, "has made all the difference."

Bob wasn't scheduled to be on the flight at Fairchild that day. But at the last minute he took the Wing Commander's place, who couldn't make it because he was escorting Sheila Widnall, Secretary of the Air Force, as she left the base. Sheila Widnall was at Fairchild that day to console the victims and families of the shooting spree at the base hospital four days earlier. It was definitely a bad week to be at Fairchild.

Bob was also flying his "fini" flight, his last B-52 flight before leaving the flying world and taking up a staff job somewhere else. It has been a tradition in the bomber squadrons (and in many other flying units as well) to celebrate this event by dousing the aviator with water, usually from a fire truck, and then toasting his or her flying with champagne. Since this was such a special occasion and since it was such a short flight (it was the final practice for the 20-minute demonstration flight at tomorrow's air show), Nan and the Wolff's family and friends were watching the flight from the aircraft parking area, waiting for them to land and celebrate his last flight.

The third flier on the B-52 that day was downstairs in the navigator's seat. He was Lieutenant Colonel Ken Huston, the Squadron Operations Officer. Ken was one of the nicest people you would ever hope to meet, and I feel fortunate to count him among my closest friends in the Air Force. Ken and I had also been stationed at Grand Forks Air Force Base together, and we had gone on to teach the Air Force Academy together. When I left the Academy to go to Oxford, Ken stayed on, and then moved to Fairchild a few years before I got there.

As navigators with roughly the same seniority, we often found ourselves in friendly competition for assignments or positions of responsibility. In 1992, we both competed for an assignment to Air Command and Staff College, a mid-level professional school in Montgomery, Alabama. One of us would leave for Alabama; the other would become the Operations Officer, second in command of the Bomb Squadron. In truth, neither one of us wanted to leave. As it turned out, I lost, and was chosen to leave. Ken became the Operations Officer at Fairchild.

Ken was on the flight that day in June because one of the younger navigators in the squadron objected to flying with Bud. Ken, as the senior navigator, had volunteered to take his place. That's the kind of guy he was.

The fourth man aboard the B-52 that day was sitting in the co-pilot's seat. He was Lieutenant Colonel Mark McGeehan, the commander of the Bomb Squadron. Mark was a fellow student of mine at Air Command and Staff College in Alabama. He left Alabama to become the commander, and shortly after he arrived he began to hear complaints about Bud Holland. Mark had no authority to ground Bud, since Bud didn't work directly for him. So he took the complaints to the Operations Group Commander, who was Bud's boss. But the Group Commander was one of those leaders who really couldn't handle bad news, especially against one of his stars. Despite Mark's repeated attempts to get the Commander to see the problem, he refused to listen. He thought Mark was failing to show the proper loyalty to a B-52 legend, who was so close to retirement. "Why hurt the man's career? That's not the way we do things in the Air Force. Bud has been loyal to us, and we have to reciprocate." In fact, at one point, the Group Commander threatened to fire Mark if he continued to make waves. "Quit worrying. It's not like Bud's going to kill anybody," he told Mark. That was about three weeks before the accident.

Without the support he needed, Mark did the next best thing he could. He directed that he be put on the schedule to fly with Bud Holland any time he was in the air. An experienced instructor pilot himself, Mark reasoned that if he were at the controls as well, at least Bud wouldn't be able to do something stupid that would get his people killed. "I can protect them," he thought. Incorrectly, as it turned out. Jesus said, "There is no greater love than this: to lay down one's life for one's friends."

The crew had completed its flying practice for the air show at about 2:00 p.m. As they came in for their final approach and landing, another aircraft had pulled onto the runway for takeoff. The B-52 was directed to come around again. So they flew a low approach over the runway at about 250 feet off the ground, standard procedure. About halfway down the runway stood the control tower. As they passed the tower, Bud Holland, who was flying the airplane at the time, began a 360-degree turn around the control tower, a la *Top Gun*.

Except he wasn't flying an F-14. It was a big, lumbering bomber with a 185-foot wingspan. The flight manuals warned pilots that banking the aircraft more than 30-degrees in normal flight operations was prohibited; going over 45-degrees of bank, even in an emergency, was not allowed. The bomber rolled through 30, then 45, then 55, 60 degrees of bank. At 65 degrees the aircraft was no longer flying—it was a missile. But it continued to roll— 75, 80, 85 degrees. At 95 degrees of bank, the nose impacted the ground, and the plane exploded into a sickening ball of flames.

No one survived. No one ejected. The accident investigation showed that only Mark McGeehan, sitting in the co-pilot's seat, had made any attempt to get out. He had moved one of the trigger handles on his ejection seat just enough to pop his ejection hatch, but there had been no time to get out. No one else had made any move, or said anything over the radio. It was all over in a heartbeat. All in plain sight of the group waiting to celebrate Bob Wolff's last flight.

———————————————————————

What went wrong is, I hope, fairly obvious.

Failed leadership.

A group commander mired in cronyism, unable to see the dangers of protecting one of his own. An organization that had clearly lost its moral compass, its true sense of purpose—its values.

We have the ingredients for a tragedy of gut-wrenching proportions. Four people dead, one airplane obliterated. And it gets worse. Following a criminal investigation, the group commander was court-martialed, but plea-bargained before the start of his trial. Under the agreement, he was allowed to retire with full pension and benefits, rather than spending time in prison for dereliction of duty. Thus justice was denied for the widows and children of the aviators who died senselessly.

As tough as this story is to tell, it is only one in a large and—sadly—growing repository of tales involving ethical lapses by leaders in all types of occupations. Stories about priests as child molesters, stories about embezzlement and philandering by the former head of

United Way, stories about vandalism and a code of silence enforced by the members of the USA men's Olympic Hockey Team at Nagano, Japan. Not every story ends with funerals, but every story is sad in its own way.

The list goes on, and we find ourselves with two possible responses to these stories: Shake our heads and ask, "How could this happen?" or sit down and ask ourselves, "How can we do better?"

I think the second question is much more productive.

Relativism

How can we do better to overcome the chronic short-sightedness which keeps us too narrowly focused on the daily grind? In other words, how can we change our focal length before *we* show up in a newspaper article and have to begin the painful process of damage control?

Well, you asked a philosopher, so the answer you're going to hear will involve some introspection. And the first part of that answer has to do with how we make ethical decisions.

Think back to what our group commander told Mark McGeehan when Mark wanted to have Bud grounded. "That's not the way we do things in the Air Force," he seemed to be saying. "Bud has been loyal to us, and we have to reciprocate."

If you happen to be a philosopher, you would label this Ethical Cultural Relativism. Fancy term for a very simple concept: We determine what is right and wrong by looking around us. If everybody's doing it, it must be right. If not, chances are it's wrong. Pretty simple. And very basic.

Relativism has been around for a very long time, and there are important aspects of it that are quite healthy. Those of us who claim to remember the 1960's will see that Relativism played a big part in the Flower Child movement: "Live and let live" provided the foundation of the peace movement; "I'm OK. You're OK" pervaded our relationships. What we said to each other was something like this: "I have a set of beliefs and so do you. I'm pretty sure mine is right, but I can never be completely certain that I have a lock on the Truth. So I will respect our differences. My beliefs are right for me and my group; yours, likewise, are right for you."

Not a bad way to live. It prevents the need for Unabombers and other terrorists. It creates a culture of inclusion, not exclusion.

However, taken to an extreme, Relativism can lead to some bizarre and dangerous results. Consider this: About two years ago, I received a survey in the mail from our school district. It seems they were considering changing the way they calculated grade point averages for high school students who took Advanced Placement courses. For those courses, they were thinking about using a "weighted grade" 5.0 scale, instead of the traditional 4.0, where an "A" would be worth 5 points, a "B" 4, and so on down the line. The idea was to reward students in those advanced classes for the extra effort. Furthermore, they wanted my opinion about the matter. I was genuinely touched. After years of using my tax money, they actually cared about what I thought.

So I immediately grabbed a pen and sat down to fill out the short questionnaire. I read the first question:

School systems which use weighted grades experience more success in admissions to highly selective colleges. Circle one: Agree Disagree

I was puzzled. The second question has to be easier, I thought. I was wrong:

School systems which use weighted grades experience more success in procuring scholarships for their students.
Circle one: Agree Disagree

I was sure the third question was going to be:

The capital of Lithuania is Riga.
Circle one: Agree Disagree

The point is that some things are simply right or wrong, regardless of what the majority of people in a Gallup survey believe.   Either weighted GPAs help with admissions and scholarships or they don't. No survey or focus group result can possibly affect the facts. To think otherwise is just absurd.

So much for the interesting theoretical problem. There is a much more practical issue. Think back to high school physics. If you took it, you may recall your physics teacher telling you that there are four fundamental forces in the universe. A good Trivial Pursuit question. The first two are relatively easy. (Sorry. No pun intended.) Gravitational and electro-magnetic forces. But now it gets tough. The other two are fairly recent discoveries.

Research physicists, some of the most phenomenal minds of our century, discovered these two at the sub-atomic level of the universe. And what names did these Nobel-worthy scientists come up with?

The Strong Force and the Weak Force.

If ever there were a group of individuals in dire need of a thesaurus...

In any case, that's what your physics teacher taught you. But of course, she was wrong. There is a more fundamental force in existence, one more powerful than all of the others combined. We call it Peer Pressure.

Those of you who have teenagers will especially be able to recognize this force of nature: "Ah, come on! How come I can't have various parts of my body pierced?! All my friends are?! It's not fair!" (Please add appropriate whining delivery.)

Yes, the bane of the teenage years! The need to fit in, be part of the group. Every generation, I suspect, has suffered from this drive. Even philosophers' kids are not immune.

My older son, Aaron, was just starting his sophomore year in high school when he turned 15. As he began that year, he came to me and said, "Dad..." (At this point I already knew I was in trouble.) "I need a car."

"You what?"

"I need a car."

"But, Aaron, you're a full year away from getting your driver's license. Why in the world are you asking me this now?"

"Well, I figured this was going to be a long negotiating process; I wanted to get started early."

This is one smart kid.

"OK, you get points for career planning. But why is it that you 'need' a car?" (I love that word, "need." Makes whatever you're asking for sound so desperate, as if lives hang in the balance.)

"Well, I'm a sophomore now. I can't ride the bus anymore. Only freshmen ride the bus. All of my friends drive to school."

("All" of them. Right up there with "need.")

"You mean no one above the level of 9th grade (with the possible exception of the driver) is *ever* on the bus? That every single one of your classmates drives to school?" (I was hearing the classic language of teenage totality. Exaggeration for convenience, especially effective in bolstering an otherwise weak argument. But I was a master of logic; Aaron wasn't going to pull this one over on me. I was going to call his bluff.) "I'll tell you what, pal. I will drive you to school tomorrow, and we'll just see if everyone in fact drives to school."

The next day we headed off together. And I discovered something: He was absolutely right. Everyone was driving to school. If you like to be scared, don't bother with Stephen King books. Drive in a high school student

parking lot at 7:00 in the morning! Terrifying. Things
have changed since we were there. It's not just a few kids
who are lucky enough to drive. It is everybody. And they
aren't driving old '57 Fords anymore. The lot is loaded.
Sport utilities. BMWs. Nothing more than a year or two
old. I definitely felt, ah, vehicle-challenged. "Something
tells me we're living in the wrong school district, Aaron."

Yes, he felt the pressure, a very real pressure, to fit in.
This is the teenage scourge. It's certainly nice to know
we outgrow it as we mature into adulthood.

Maybe.

Consider this situation: You're driving the interstate that
runs through your nearest good-sized city. The San Diego
Freeway through Los Angeles; the Dan Ryan through
Chicago; the Beltway in Washington; or maybe just I-25
in Colorado Springs. And (of course) you're doing the
speed limit. Now let's say that a lone car passes you.
Whoosh. If you're like most of us, your reaction is
perhaps something like: "Idiot! Go! Who cares? I hope
there's a state trooper waiting around the corner." In the

heyday of CB's, drivers like that were called "bear bait." Maybe they still are.

OK, so far, so good. (Except there's no state trooper; never is, when you "need" them.) Now let's say the situation changes. You're still doing the speed limit and four cars pass you. *WhooshWhooshWhooshWhoosh.* Now what's your reaction? You feel that right foot getting just a little heavier. Don't feel too bad; it's pretty natural.

See, we drive the interstate like lemmings, where the pack mentality rules. Just get lost in the crowd, and no one (like, for instance, the state trooper who *will* be there now) will notice your behavior. Glance down at your speedometer the next time you find yourself in traffic like that and I think you'll be amazed. Or better yet, keep driving the speed limit. You will really be amazed at how people treat you. "How dare you obey the law when nobody else is!" That's what that sign language means.

Peer Pressure. What a force. Peer Pressure will make us do things that, at a later date, we can only shake our heads at, wondering at our sheer stupidity. Just take a stroll

back through your teens and early twenties. Remember
that party, that dare, that narrow escape? OK, OK,
enough, come back to reality now! But think about why
you did it.

"Because all my friends did it."

Great logic.

Try to visualize Peer Pressure like this: When I was going
through Navigator Flight Training I lived in Sacramento.
On Sunday afternoons when we had nothing better to do,
we would grab inner tubes, towels, bathing suits and six-
packs of, ah, I'm sure it must have been some sort of diet
cola! In any case, we'd head out to the American River,
which at that point is probably no more than 100 yards
across, maybe waist deep at the center, with a few rocks,
but no serious white water. We would lay back in those
inner tubes and float. As I look out at the snow falling
and drifting around my Colorado Springs home today, I
remember quite fondly that cobalt blue California sky,
85° temperatures, a slight breeze wafting against my
face. Just floating down the river, lying there getting skin
cancer, but who cared? Life was good. That is, unless

you had to go back upstream for some reason, say one of your colas got away. So you'd hop out into the water and start upstream. Only at that point did you realize what a powerful force that river was. Unless you had incredible leg strength, you basically had only two choices: go with the flow, or get out, and walk along the shore.

Peer Pressure is a river just like that. Most of us, most of the time, have no idea we are subject to its current. But we are. Psychologists call it the need for external validation, the need to fit in, from something as mundane as what to wear, to something more sinister, like what to think. Political experts play on that, trumpeting public opinion polling numbers that favor their position or candidate, hoping for a "bandwagon" effect. More often like a feeding frenzy.

And life is good as long as you're going with the flow. But imagine a situation where everyone around you is telling you to do something you know in your heart is wrong. Unless you are gifted with some serious personal strength—which we call moral courage—you have only two choices: go with the flow, or get out, find a new job.

Despite its few positive points, I tell you about Relativism, not because it's the best way to handle moral decisions, but because it's rampant. It is alive and well in your business, your church, your school, your community. To guard against being swept along with the tide against your better judgment, you must be aware that the tide exists. Or the flow will take you where you don't want to be.

Egoism

Clearly Relativism as a way of solving your ethical problems is not enough. The danger of "group-think" is too real. Independent thinking is an antidote for this deficiency, since it helps you evaluate a situation more rationally, without the risk of being swept along with the wrong flow.

But independent thinking by itself is not enough either. Without something more fundamental, simply avoiding the flow may lead to an equally flawed way of thinking: Egoism.

Here is yet another one of those fancy philosophical words for a very simple—and all too familiar—way of looking at life. Egoism claims that "right" is anything in my own best interest, and "wrong" is anything that is not. Simple idea, and it seems to fit well with our human nature. In fact, the early 17th Century English philosopher, Thomas Hobbes, believed that we couldn't help but act in our own best interest—"looking out for Number 1" was part of our genetic makeup.

There are a number of juicy philosophical issues to be debated about Egoism, such as: How do we know what's in our best interest if we can't see the future? Are we talking about short-term or long-term best interest? Isn't anything I do that helps someone else also in my best interest too? The list goes on, but I want to steer clear of these issues, mostly because I promised you that this book wouldn't degenerate into some dusty philosophy treatise.

Instead, I want to focus on one aspect of Egoism—its emphasis on the bottom line. "What's in it for me?" as a motto for egoism points out that the end result is really all that matters. How I accomplish my goals really doesn't matter that much. Did I max out my own happiness? If so, I done good! End of discussion.

This is a double-barreled problem. When I think like an egoist, not only do I ignore the needs, desires and concerns of those around me—those who are affected by what I do—but I also focus only on the outcome, the results of my decisions and actions. Usually while ignoring the methods I'm going to use to get to that goal. "Winning isn't everything; it's the only thing." "Just do it." "The ends justify the means." You can fill in your own version of the results-only fixation.

Familiar, but ethically risky thinking. There are as many examples of how disastrous this can be as there are ways of describing it. Slavery. Expansion of the American West. Sherman's March to the Sea. Watergate. Use of steroids and other illegal substances. Lieutenant Colonel Oliver North and the Iran-Contra Affair. It doesn't matter how you get the job done, as long as you reach your goal.

But the price does matter. The ends don't justify the means. Ends and means must both be justified. How we do what we do is every bit as important as what we accomplish. Without that, we cannot be distinguished from farm animals.

Here's the problem with bottom-line thinking, particularly when it's self-centered (as it so often is), and especially when it's the short-term bottom line that we're after (which, again, it usually is). It has to do with one of the intriguing words in ethics: Integrity.

One of the most challenging things about speaking to audiences about ethics is coming up with an adjective form of the word Integrity. Think about it: The whole concept of adjectives first forced itself upon you in sixth grade grammar. I remember that. All too well! I had a teacher who would have made the Grand Inquisitor blush. She was tough. No corporal punishment, but the psychological abuse she could dish out if you crossed her (which I did on a goodly number of occasions) was brutal. She was a nun, but clearly not one of the Sisters of Mercy.

Sister "Rasputin" taught me grammar. And I didn't soon forget those lessons! In particular, she taught me about the difference between the noun and adjective forms of a word. Structurally, they have the same root, but they have different endings. Adjective forms end in "al" or "an" or "ous" or something like that.

So using the information that Sister R. armed me with, what is the adjective form of the word, "integrity"? The most likely candidate has got to be "integral".

Yuck.

Welcome to calculus class. That's where you'll find integral. That stylized mathematical operator that looked just a little like an f. The very thing that drove me into philosophy! Now as an adjective risen from the dead to haunt me. The etymology gods (surely there must be such things) are laughing at the cruel joke that forces me in front of audiences awaiting with the sage advice: "Be integral!" Oh, yeah, that's worth hearing!

But there's more to the grammar lesson. And the math lesson. There's another word similar to integral that floats around the math class and gives us the real clue to the meaning of integrity. Integer. Now there's a word you probably first encountered in grade school. And no doubt you well remember that an integer is a *whole number*. Like 1, 2, 3 and so on.

Armed with that piece of trivia, we can now see the real meaning of integrity. It is *wholeness of character*. Of who we are. Integrity is not, as some people think, synonymous with honesty. Without a doubt honesty is a big part of integrity. So is forthrightness. And courage.

But integrity is more than these. Let me explain it this way:

Imagine that you are looking at a concrete post. A good, sturdy post. Well constructed. Maybe 3½ feet high, 6 inches in diameter. The kind you see so often in front of drive-up windows or in front of supermarkets.

Now imagine I have been given the job of removing that post. Tough job, but I think I can handle it. Where are my tools? Do I get a jack hammer? No. How about a winch? Or a chain and a bulldozer? Nope.

All I have is a sledgehammer. Twelve-pound head. Good solid oak handle. A perfect tool. So I get started. I grab that sledgehammer and take a shot at that post. I hit it as absolutely hard as I can. Boom! With very, very little effect. At least on the post. I've recoiled from the shock of the blow. The post suffers maybe one small chunk for all my efforts.

So I take a second shot at the post. With similar results. Another little chunk goes flying off.

But I don't quit. I keep slamming that post. And an interesting thing begins to happen. The more I hit it, the weaker the internal structure of the concrete becomes. And each time bigger and bigger chunks go flying off.

Chunk.

Chunk.

Chunk.

And it's not all that long before I'm standing over a pile of concrete dust. Mission accomplished.

So let's connect this to integrity. Our character is just like that concrete post. Strong, sturdy, rigid. But life is full of sledgehammers. Every time we give in to the flow of the Peer Pressure River when we know it's not the right thing to do, every time we succumb to the temptation to go after short-term, egoistic bottom lines when we really know better, we run a serious risk. We risk the hammer.

Chunk.

Chunk.

Chunk.

It's in the little things, in those moments where we convince ourselves that "Nobody will ever know," that we run the greatest risk. Because at least one person will always know. Always. And that's the very person who will never let you forget. You.

Chunk.

Chunk.

Chunk.

Here's the question: How many shots from the hammer can we take before we're a pile of character dust, blowing in the wind? I don't know the answer to that question, but I don't think we're quite as strong as concrete.

Here's some good news: When I described that concrete post to you, I wasn't completely accurate. The ones in front of drive-up windows aren't plain concrete any more.

Engineers have redesigned them—they are now concrete encased in a steel pipe. These crafty engineers know that concrete protected with steel won't chunk.

Integrity is the ability to resist chunking. It's like a steel pipe protecting your character. The bad news is that you can't put on integrity in one motion. It goes on a teaspoon at a time. Each time you refuse to give in to the temptation to chunk, you get stronger, and it gets easier to say "No" the next time.

And there will be a next time. The sledgehammer is relentless.

But you can become *hammer-proof.*

A Leader's Role:
Character Development

Now about this point, you may be thinking: "This is a *positive* approach to ethics and leadership? Aircrew members annihilated in a ball of flame? A despondent mother of two puts a shotgun to her head? I'm swept along with the Peer Pressure River, while chunking under the relentless attack of the sledgehammer? I wonder what this guy's *negative* approach looks like?"

Well, it has been pretty bleak. So far. But that's about to change. Because you can make a difference in all this. That's what I told you at the beginning, and now I'm going to show you how.

The first thing we need to do is stop focusing on you as an individual, and take a look at your role as a leader in your organization. Which you are, no matter what you do there.

So, as a leader, if I were to ask you what type of people you want working for and with you, I'm guessing you would say that you want the sort of people who do the right thing almost instinctively, almost by habit. They do right, regardless of whether the *New York Times* will get the story or whether there's a state patrol car in the lane beside them. In other words, you want people of high integrity.

So I'm going to do a little experiment right now. I'm going to give you two examples of people (from articles I recently found in the Colorado Springs *Gazette*) and I want you to think about which type you want working with you. (Hint: Remember I told you nothing in this book would be complicated. Well, I don't think you'll have to consult a rocket scientist to figure this one out.)

Example 1: Greased Lightning

The Denver Broncos were Super Bowl Champions in 1998, and along the way they beat the Kansas City Chiefs (in Kansas City) to advance to the AFC Championship games. Following the game, NFL officials fined five of the Bronco offensive linemen $5000 each for smearing Vaseline on their uniform jerseys to keep the Chiefs' defenders from getting a hold of them. Part way through the first quarter, one of the referees spotted excessive amounts of Vaseline on the jerseys and had them go to the sidelines to clean it off. In a media interview the following week, some of the Broncos expressed their displeasure with the league decision. Mike Lodish said that "use of Vaseline among offensive linemen is as common as profanity." (Interesting comparison in and of itself) Lodish went on to say, "This is ludicrous. Everybody uses it." (Sound familiar? Glance back at the chapter on Relativism, and teenagers.) Fullback Howard Griffith had this to say: "The key is not to get caught. They got caught. That's the bottom line. Everybody's looking for an edge. That's what it's all about." The key is not to get caught.

Example 2: Some Days are Diamonds

In July of 1997, Laura Vannoy made a move from Steamboat Springs, Colorado, to Denver. During the move, she misplaced eight black velvet bags containing $38,000 worth of unset diamonds. She was sure they were gone forever. But she was wrong. You see, she had hired a cleaning crew of three employees from a company called Clean Living in Steamboat Springs to clean her house in preparation for closing. During the final cleaning inspection by the crew, they discovered the eight velvet bags and their sparkling contents in a kitchen drawer. Recalling the incident later, one of the workers said this: "We didn't know how much they were worth at the time, but we were all wide eyed." Then came the kicker: "We didn't think twice about returning the gems. We go into people's homes on a daily basis, and people trust us with their prized possessions. We knew right away we had to return them."

I love that. "We didn't think twice."

I told you this wouldn't be a real tough test.

See, what we want from our colleagues is commitment, not merely compliance. And what this means is good people, not just good actions (sometimes) or good results (even most of the time). But the real trick is ensuring that you have good people. Tough challenge. If you own a major league sports team, I suppose you can buy good people. Well, OK, maybe not good people, but certainly good athletes. However, purchasing employees is usually not the best option.

The key for you is to foster the right sort of ethical climate in your organization, the kind of climate in which people are rewarded for doing the right thing. If you want instinctively good behavior, you need to set up an organizational environment in which people can practice and develop the right sort of behavioral habit patterns. Aristotle, foremost among the ancient Greek philosophers, understood this strong connection between habitual behavior and ethics quite well. His *Nicomachean Ethics* is a description, not of right acts, but of good people. In fact, the Greek word for "habit" is *ethiké*, from which we get the word, "ethics."

The Woodstock Theological Center published a short monograph in 1990 entitled, "Creating and Maintaining an Ethical Corporate Climate," which was the result of a conference of academicians and major business executives. Their final report had this to say about business leaders (you): "Their task becomes one of creating a workplace climate in which ethics is so integral to day-to-day operations that ethical behavior is *virtually self-enforcing.*" And they go on to issue this warning:

> Ethical behavior in business is not simply a matter of the character and virtue of each individual involved in a business enterprise. It is also a product of, and a contributor to, the ethical climate in which that firm operates. In fact, many benefits of individual good deeds *may be lost if they are not supported by a strong ethical climate.*

To understand what this means, think about the Peer Pressure River: What if you have only one good employee, one person who wants to do the right thing? What are her choices against the current of that river? Only two: go with the flow (even though it's wrong), or get out.

But before you get completely depressed, here's the good news: Imagine that you have an organization in which the River is flowing the right direction, in which people are rewarded for doing the right thing, a climate which is conducive to developing the right habit patterns. Now add into that environment one bad apple, one employee who is doing the wrong thing. What are his choices? The same two: go with the (right) flow, or get out. Now you have employees saying to each other, "Hey, we don't do that sort of thing here. Get with the program." Imagine what happens to your discipline problem rate—it drops out of sight. Your managers and supervisors are no longer stuck in the 95-5 hole: spending 95% of their time on 5% of their employees.

Now, think about your role in creating this change: What is the Peer Pressure River made of? Nothing but people, and you (as a leader) are at the head of the River. You can't eliminate Peer Pressure, but you can do something much better—*leverage* it to your advantage. Put ethical thinking into the very fabric of your organization, and change the flow. You can do this. Indeed, if not you, who can?

To do this, you need to know what ethical thinking looks like. First, you begin at the very heart of your organization.

Think for a moment about what drives you to work as hard as you do? It can't be money alone, not just about the financial bottom line. It has got to be something more, something deeper, something about values.

Values are the key here. Values are what we ultimately strive for, and they're bigger than mere financial rewards. They are about being a part of some activity or some purpose larger than ourselves. In any organization, values are the foundational beliefs about what is fundamentally important. Put another way, values are the bedrock upon which the organization is built; they are its soul. From a personal standpoint, values are the anchors that keep you from going with the flow in the Peer Pressure River.

Values come in many different varieties, and in varying hierarchical order. They include concepts like integrity, honesty, fairness, excellence, service, and respect for other beings and the world around us.

Used correctly (that is, not merely stuck on a poster in the break room), values are the real bottom line—every decision, every policy must eventually be grounded in, come down to, the central values.

If a decision cannot easily be traced back to the organizational values, it's a bad decision. Simple as that.

What are your values? If they have never been articulated, it would be well worth the time spent doing so.

Here's an example: A few years ago, when John Anderson (a big proponent of values-based leadership) was elected Sheriff of El Paso County, Colorado, and head of the 500-plus employees and deputies of the El Paso County Sheriff's Office, one of his first official acts was to establish the organizational core values of Honesty, Loyalty and Unity, and the motto—Service with Honor All deputies now wear those words on their uniform sleeve patch as a reminder to them and the members of the community they serve. And they're not just a fancy public relations ploy: All policy decisions are made with those values in mind.

But when it comes to organizational climate change, the real question is this: What do you do with those values on a daily basis to create change?

Well, there is only one way, and it's extremely simple: As a leader, the way you develop those around you, the way you nurture people to become habitually good, is by example. By your personal attitude and behavior.

You have heard the cliché that "you can't just talk the talk, you have to walk the talk." Nice idea, but it doesn't go far enough. In developing by example, you cannot just walk the talk—you have to *live* the talk, you have to *be* the talk. Gandhi said it this way: "Be the change you want to see in the world." That is the true essence of leadership.

What's more, if you publicly ascribe to a set of values (either by creating them for your company or accepting its stated values), and yet do not act in a way consistent with them, you have entered the realm of hypocrisy. One of my favorite alternative definitions of "integrity" is "a consistency in what you value, what you say and what you do." In an essay called "Social Aims," Ralph Waldo Emerson was pretty blunt about this: "Don't *say* things. What you *are* stands over you the while, and thunders so that I cannot hear what you say to the contrary."

Employees are almost as good as children at spotting hypocrisy.

On the other hand, if you are consistent in your actions—in the little things as well as the big ones—you will begin to develop genuine, lasting character improvements in those around you.

Make no mistake: Gaining commitment from your colleagues is hard work. Unfortunately, gaining compliance—from our children as well as from our co-workers—is always much easier. It doesn't take much interpersonal skill to yell and scream to get things done the way you want. Your 9-year old will begin to clean up her room if you stand there watching, arms crossed, foot insistently tapping. And she will comply with your demands, as long as you continue to monitor her progress. But get bored and leave, even with a "Keep going. I'll be back in 15 minutes and I want this place spotless" thrown over your shoulder, and you know exactly what will happen. Work stoppage. Those workers you supervise are no different, especially if you treat them no differently, as you practice "seagull" leadership: fly in, make a lot of noise, dump on everyone, fly out.

Developmental leadership is much more of a challenge, just like effective parenting. But it's not as hard as it first appears, and here's why: They're watching.

When I first joined the teaching faculty at the United States Air Force Academy in 1985, my department head was Colonel (now General) Malham Wakin. Very early on, he sat me down and explained something to me. (It was the first of many mentoring conversations we would have over the years, for which I am a much better person.) "Wherever you go in Colorado Springs," he told me, "a cadet will be watching you. In the classroom (when they're awake) they'll be observing you. When you walk down the hall, a cadet will be behind you, watching.

"But there's more than that: When you're waiting for a table at a restaurant and you make a scene because you should have been seated 30 minutes ago, a cadet will be in the restaurant with you, watching. When you angrily cut off another driver on the interstate because he didn't signal or wasn't going fast enough, a cadet will be in a car nearby, watching. When you get into the 10-items-or-less express lane at the super market with 12 items, a cadet will be behind you, counting. When the cashier (his name is "Trainee") inadvertently gives you $10 too much in change, and you know it but don't say anything, there will be a cadet in line with you (who happens to be a math major) counting even faster than you did."

That made a big impression on me. I was only a captain at the time, a junior officer on a faculty of 550 officers. And yet I was being watched. I have to tell you it made me a bit nervous.

Now think about your own situation. No doubt you have a lot more visibility in your organization than I did. How does the line go? "You can run, but you can't hide." Everywhere you go, somebody will know somebody who knows you, and the word will circulate.

This bit of information could either scare the heck out of you or thrill you. I guess it depends on what you do when you think nobody is watching. It will thrill you if you remember how you go about changing the climate in your organization: by example. What this means is you don't have to work very hard to make a BIG impact on the River. Somebody is always watching when you come up on an ethical yellow light. Especially, as luck would have it, when you give in to the pounding of that sledgehammer, and you chunk. Remember this:

> ### WARNING
> *Chunking as a leader is highly contagious.*

Your behavior as a leader validates the behavior of those you lead. Crack, and everyone around you will follow suit. But resisting the hammer, refusing to give in, is also highly contagious. They will watch you, and they will learn by observing.

So if you want to make a positive impact on your ethical environment, use your values in practical decision making every day. And you will be a positive example for the ethical development of those around you (both below and above you in the corporate food chain).

If you have gotten this so far, all you need to know is how to do it. Before I give you some practical advice, I need to deal with one nagging issue: Accountability.

Accountability:

The Flip-Side of Character Development

So you've worked—struggled really—to get your organization to the point where the River is flowing in the right direction. Your folks are sending positive messages to each other about how the core values play out in the workplace every day. Supervisors are reporting a conspicuous lack of disciplinary problems with the employees. Incidents of sick leave abuse, late arrivals, and antagonism reflect a notable downward trend. Things are going quite well.

Almost.

You still have a small percentage of problem workers. Just a few who just don't seem to get it, who haven't "bought into" the organization's values. The more rope you give them, the harder they seem to pull. For whatever reason, they seem hell-bent on going against the positive flow of the River. Mentoring doesn't work; positive messages seem to be ignored. It's only a matter of time before they get into serious trouble.

What now?

One of the hardest problems for many leaders to face is accountability: Ensuring those you lead maintain at least the minimum organizational standard. And doling out the consequences if they don't. It's hard because the consequences, as you realize, are discipline or dismissal (or jail, should the problem be bad enough). It's also hard because correcting behavioral problems without anger— and with empathy—often takes all the interpersonal skills we have, and more.

Accountability is the flip side of nurturing. You may well do your very best to create the right sort of ethical climate, to develop those under you into tomorrow's leaders by your consistent, positive example. Yet there will likely always be a few who don't get it.

Without apology, I admit to my unwavering, naïve optimism about the nature of the human spirit—that each of us has within us the great capacity for goodness, the capacity to rise up to meet the exhibited goodness in our fellow human beings. I believe this is part of our genetic makeup, hardwired into us over millions of years of evolution. It is the same wiring that gives the ability to empathize, to see and feel things from someone else's point of view.

I'm not oblivious to reality. Of course I know that newspapers are daily filled with evidence which should whither my optimism. This book too contains its share of appalling examples of outrageously bad ethical behavior. Yet, here I stand (as Martin Luther put it). Just the very fact that bad things are still newsworthy bolsters my faith in humankind and should be some comfort to you pessimists. At least at this point in our cultural evolution, bad behavior is not *that* commonplace.

But you still can't reach everybody. What then? Well, you could resort to the old model of seagull leadership and compliance: Beat them until they conform! But you and I both know that just doesn't work. It doesn't work at home as a parent. It certainly won't work in the business world.

Which is not to say that you can't have standards and accountability. The key here is that you and your associates must be accountable, but that doesn't mean you all must be *held* accountable. Notice the slight but important difference here. To *be accountable* is to accept responsibility for your *own* actions. It is an internal attitude—a mark of maturity. In philosophical terms, to be accountable is to be *autonomous*, self-governed, self-contained. On the other hand to be *held◦accountable* implies being controlled by someone else, an external force, that is, being *heteronomous*. If I am held accountable, I don't have to accept responsibility for my own actions. Instead I surrender that power to another.

Big difference. Really the same difference we saw earlier between compliance and commitment, the Denver Broncos and the Clean Living cleaning crew. Doing something because you have to versus doing something because you want to.

So what you want is a way to ensure that your associates are accountable without holding them so, especially with the issue of discipline. Here I take a page or two from the work of my famous brother, Dr. J. Zink, the family therapist. Those of you familiar with his work know that J. makes an important distinction between punishments and prices. Your daughter holds you hostage to social blackmail in the supermarket, threatening a major scene right there in the candy aisle unless you let her have the 3-pound bag of Snickers bars (which, a part of your brain says, doesn't look too bad). Resisting your own temptation, you refuse to be coerced, and the scene begins, resulting in every head in the store turning in your direction to witness some outrageous form of child abuse, judging from the screams emanating from your daughter. The real issue is how you handle the aftermath, when you get her home (without the Snickers).

Response 1: You launch into a retaliatory tirade of your own ("Do you know how you embarrassed me in the store? How could you do such a thing to me? Get out of my sight!").

Response 2: You remind her of the consequences for making a bad choice (which—good Zink

> Method parent that you are—you had
> already established ahead of time). She
> accepts (maybe reluctantly) the
> consequences, because it was her choice.

The difference in your two responses lies in how your daughter feels *about herself* afterward. Her reaction to Response 1 is something like this: "I'm a bad person, and I'm in trouble." Compare that to the reaction to Response 2: "Oops. I made a bad choice that time. But I'm still a good person. Mommy and I can work together to make sure the same thing doesn't happen again."

J. calls this the difference between punishments and prices. Punishments are designed to make us feel bad about ourselves. They inflict pain. They tear at our basic human dignity and worth. Coming from someone we look up to (parent or boss), they can be devastating. Prices, on the other hand, are what we pay for the choices we make. They don't inflict pain; they incur costs. In psycho-economic terms (if there are such things), they are the result, the downside of a cost-benefit analysis. As such, they promote rational thinking, especially in kids. They uphold our basic human worth. The traffic cop who stops you for speeding has you pay a price for your bad choice. She certainly doesn't humiliate you (punish you) for that choice.

When we *hold* people accountable for their actions, we punish them for doing wrong, and the psychological deadspin begins. On the other hand, when we create an organizational climate in which people *are* accountable for their actions, they know they will pay a price for their bad choices. By doing so, we give them an opportunity to rise up and accept personal accountability, something very different from the debilitating fear of external punishment.

Think about how this connects with the issues of privacy and trust in the workplace: Employees who are heteronomous—held in compliance of company policies—quickly develop a mindset in which the goal is to *get away* with things—to avoid getting caught. Remember, if I am *held accountable* it means that I am under external control. Human nature being what it is, that means my natural tendency will be to figure out ways of circumventing that control, that authority. This spawns a sort of POW camp mentality where I view my boss and the hierarchy supporting her as the *enemy* to be defeated.

Beating the system becomes an important part of my behavior pattern, a game, an obsession.

If those above me or around me foster a workplace climate that is externally compliance-driven, I will find myself in exactly the wrong type of ethical environment—poisoning, not nurturing; punishing, not rewarding.

Now add to this equation the Peer Pressure River: The POW mentality will spread like wildfire. It will be us, the oppressed workers, against them, the tyrannical establishment. This is the sort of climate in which labor disputes fester ("We have to stick together no matter what the long-term negative consequences are to our employer"), where employee theft is a constant problem ("I'm just getting even, getting what I deserve"), where turnover rates are brutally high ("I don't need this; I'm out of here!").

So commitment is the key. And that leaves us exactly where we want to be on the question of discipline. You will still have some behavior and attitude problems, no matter how good your River is. But you will avoid the contagious bad feelings if we once again take the cue from Dr. J:

✓ Make sure the corporate policies are well publicized and clearly understood by all of your associates.

✓ Keep them as simple as possible (just like the rules for good behavior for your children).

✓ Make sure the consequences for breaking the rules (the prices) and for *living by* them (the rewards) are well understood and consistently applied.

✓ And most importantly, make sure that the consequences are definitely understood as prices, not punishments, and that those who are charged with enforcing the rules treat their fellow employees with genuine respect and dignity.

Of course this will not eliminate all of your personnel problems, but it very likely will reduce the chance of spin-off problems.

Without a doubt, you have to develop and maintain an effective system of accountability. Without it, employees will wander about aimlessly, looking for the fences, the parameters within which they can conduct themselves while trusting their fellow employees to do the same.

Accountability is the flip side of character development. An organization which creates and maintains an ethical climate that minimizes the real or perceived pressure to go against what is right is an organization which also encourages personal growth—including accepting responsibility for one's attitudes and behaviors. Equitable and consistent enforcement of well conceived, values-based rules and policies will send a powerful, positive message that supervisors and managers in this organization can be trusted to "live the talk," and rest assured that this message will get through. That in itself will go a long way to preventing the sorts of problems that generate the discussion of rules and prices. Catch 'em being good, because that's all you will be able to find!

Some Practical Advice

"So What Should I DO?"

So far, much of what I've discussed is pretty theoretical, interesting but not loaded with practical applicability. And if I left you with nothing practical, I would have failed to reach the goal I set at the beginning: to show you that ethics and values-based thinking does in fact make a difference in the success of your organization, and you, as a leader, are the key to that difference. So I can't stop yet, because I would be breaking my promise to you, and *that* wouldn't be very ethical at all.

So what can you do today to develop the kind of everyday, "steel pipe" integrity that will help you and your organization avoid the danger of chunking?

Like much of this book, the advice is pretty simple. (1 told you at the beginning this wasn't a textbook in rocket

science.)   It's a three-step process for personal and
professional integrity:

STEP 1: THINK

Practical integrity isn't an accident; it doesn't just happen.
People of high moral character, people you look up to,
have gotten to that point deliberately. And "deliberately"
is exactly the right word choice here: It means to "take
careful thought; to reflect," which is the first step to
practical integrity.

When you think, use this as a guide: Many companies, as
we have seen, have a set of organizational core values,
either stated or implied. (These values should be stated.
If yours aren't, call me. We'll talk.) Unfortunately, like
many of the best-intentioned corporate initiatives, the
values statements are carefully planned, hotly debated and
eventually agreed to (usually by some group of senior
executives). And then promptly ignored. Sure, they may
appear on your stationery, or on your PR boilerplate, or
on a poster in the break room. But no further effort is
made to understand them and their role in shaping the

organization's daily activities. They just sit there, receding into the background noise.

In the year before I retired from the Air Force, I worked with another lieutenant colonel philosopher, Pat Tower, to produce a readable, portable handbook on our values, called *The United States Air Force Core Values.* (Okay, I didn't really work *with* him. I just watched in awe and encouraged him as he single-handedly wrote the brilliantly concise document that became the centerpiece for values-based thinking in the Air Force. I was just happy to be his caddy in that endeavor.) The booklet was purposely designed to fit in a pocket or purse, ready at a moment's notice to offer inspiration and guidance in making ethical decisions. Every commander from the Chief of Staff on down loved it, and eventually over 600,000 copies were printed.

It was and is the definitive source for values thinking in the Air Force. But it was and is absolutely worthless to anyone who refuses to take the few minutes necessary to think about what the core values really mean in his or her job, whether that was financial management or anti-satellite warfare.

The same is true for your organization's core values. They literally aren't worth the paper they're written on if you don't take the time to think about them, and apply them to your particular job, whether it's widget inspection or customer relations, budget planning or strategic marketing.

That's what I want you to think about. Ask yourself, "How do our values affect us, every day? Are they (as we talked about earlier) at the root of every decision this company makes? Are they at the root of every decision *I* make, every day? Can I do better?"

Think about the larger and practical implications of what you do for a living. Consider questions like this: When Wayne Calloway, a former CEO of PepsiCo Inc., was asked why his company wasn't pulling out of Burma, given its oppressive political regime, he replied, "I don't think corporate CEOs should make foreign policy decisions." Aside from the question whether it is better for companies to disengage in such a situation, is he right? Can you afford to bury your head in the sand?

When should you do this thinking? Well, I'll tell you when the worst time is: When you're at your desk, in the office, on the job site, completely absorbed in what you do. Bad time. You don't have the psychic energy to consider the bigger picture.

So the best time to think is any other time. Away from the office. On the commute. In the shower. Over your morning cup of coffee (instead of reading the paper, or the overnight reports from your international offices). You get the idea. Give yourself a golden opportunity—let your mind wander through your occupation unobstructed. You'll be surprised what you can see. Now you have the chance to make those organizational values your own. Put them into practice. Visualize the upcoming chokepoints and how you're going to handle them.

Visualize. Not long ago, I had the opportunity to go through a team building and personal growth workshop that included a high ropes course. Given what you know about my military flying background, you might find this hard to believe, but I'm terrified of heights. Stepladders are about my upper limit. Yet this course required me to put my fear to the test in an environment in which my

rational mind knew that I was perfectly safe, but my
irrational emotions were screaming warnings at me. "How
do you know the ropes won't break?   Oh, sure they
haven't yet, but that just means they're overdue.   What,
you're going to take their word for it?   They've got it
easy—they're on the ground, which is where you ought to
be!"

Stifling those mental tapes, I took on the challenge.   The
first was climbing a 25-foot telephone pole, then standing
on a 14-inch disk loosely nailed to the top of the pole,
turning around 180 degrees, and leaping off.   No sweat.
As I stood at the base of that pole being cheered on by my
teammates ("These people don't know you or care about
you.   They're waiting to see the splat!"), my mind
continued this argument with itself, paralyzing me.

Into this cacophony of conflicting messages stepped
Eloise Levitt, a fellow participant and someone whom I
had known for about 12 hours at that point. She got in my
face in order to block everything else out.   Then she said,
"You can do this." "No, I can't," I shot back.   Without a
pause, she answered, "Yes. You can.   Just close your eyes
and visualize yourself at the top of the pole.   Visualize it

all, the sights, the sounds, the smells, but most of all the feeling of complete victory. Do you like that feeling? Well, start climbing and it's yours."

That was all I needed. I went straight to the top and experienced the exhilarating rush of success. And I knew exactly what it would feel like because I rehearsed the entire experience in my head before I left the ground.

That's the importance of visualizing the ethical chokepoints. You mentally experience the upcoming events and plan your course of action in response. This is the only way downhill skiers can excel at their sport (or survive, for that matter). Hurtling down the side of what is in effect an ice-covered vertical wall is just not the time to consider which way you should turn. And you know better than I that the ice-wall is your work environment. Events occur at lightning speed. Without pre-planning, ethics and values-based thinking will disappear in a heartbeat. If you want this ethics stuff to work, you must commit to some effective thinking time *before* you really need it.

Think about who you are, and what your organization is and stands for. Think about the people who interact with you, the people you care for and the people you don't care for—and why.

Do this and the first thing you're likely to discover—or re-discover—is that ethical issues impact virtually every aspect of your life. And that should make sense, remembering that the two great spheres of ethics are the people in your life (including yourself) and the environment in which you live. What else is there?

As you reflect, translate the frameworks of ethics into practice. Take what you have learned here and apply it to the real issues of your life. Obviously, I can't give you a checklist for how to be good. But you can. You know full well the issues and problems affecting your company, your family, your friends. And only you know how to "live the talk, to be the talk" as a leader in all of those realms. Only you know the ethical climate that surrounds you. And only you know the types of nurturing development needed by those you lead. Peer into the future (as a leader, you are a visionary) and ask yourself about the upcoming choke points.

And ask yourself what you can do to send powerful, positive messages, rippling likes shock waves through your organization and your world. Listen to this example: Roger Enrico, who is (at the time I'm writing this) the *current* CEO of Pepsico, Inc., is giving up $1 million of his salary to fund scholarships for the children of his front-line employees—salespeople, warehouse workers, truck drivers. In his case, that amounts to one third of his salary and benefit package. Think about the power of the message he is sending out: "I care about you, and your families, and I'm saying it in a way that counts." Awesome.

Thinking is the first step in leading by example. This is where we begin to see what an influence great character can be.

STEP 2: TALK

I've said earlier that it isn't enough to "talk the talk." But this doesn't imply that talking is useless. On the contrary, talking about the ethical aspects and issues within your organization is vital to ensure the right climate. Tom Petzinger, writing in the *Wall Street Journal*, said this: "It is axiomatic that the more often ethics are discussed, the more powerful they become."

I'm not sure that's an axiom (something we accept without any proof), but it is a very potent reminder about the practical value of keeping ethical considerations always bubbling on the front burner. Because integrity may not seem to have a direct, immediate impact on the bottom line, it can easily be marginalized, pushed aside by more pressing concerns.

And the risk of this happening is even greater during crises. In commenting on the events of World War I, California Senator Hiram Johnson noted that "the first casualty when war comes is truth." I don't know if he was right about that, but I think we can paraphrase him like this: *The first casualty when a crisis comes is integrity.*

The best way—maybe the only way—to prevent that casualty is to keep ethics at the forefront of your organization, in the little things. Because when you talk and practice integrity in the little things, doing so in the big ones—in the crises—will be easier because it will be a matter of habit. But fail to keep ethical thinking at your fingertips on a daily basis, and you may well find yourself unprepared when the big storms hit—and they will hit.

Talk to your peers, talk to your boss. Ask the tough questions about whether a particular policy or tactical move is consistent with your organization's central values. Talk to those you supervise about how the values really make a difference in your job—and theirs. And (thank you, Dr. J.) *catch 'em being good!* Make a big, sincere deal out of it. You'll be amazed at the power of this gesture. It works with your kids, and it certainly works with your compatriots on the job.

STEP 3: ACT

So you've thought through the ethical implications of what you do for a living, and you've worked hard to keep discussions and debate grounded in the values of your organization. Will any of this make any difference?

No. Not unless you follow through, and you act on your
deliberations. You see, all this talk about ethics and
integrity is truly academic (in the worst sense of that
word) unless you *do something* with it. Unless you use it
in a meaningful way to make decisions and act on them.

Aristotle claimed that ethics was a special type of
knowledge, knowledge that required practice to be of any
use. Kind of like the knowledge of how to drive a car.
When our son, Aaron, was learning to drive (almost a
year *after* he asked for a car—which, by the way, he
never got), I remember him being frustrated at the hours
of studying he had to put in, learning the driver's manual
and reading the countless articles we gave him about
driving (usually about the dangers of teenage driving).
He didn't want to read, he wanted to get behind the
wheel!

In a sense, I understood his frustration. Although the
material he was studying was important, he really
couldn't begin to learn to drive until he actually practiced
it. Every skill (the ancient Greeks called it a *techné*) is
like that—driving, golf, video games, neuro-surgery. You
can't get proficient until you get some hands-on time.

Practical integrity is no different. Thinking about it, talking about it is just not enough. You've got to get out there and try it. But just like driving, it's wise to start easy, where the challenges aren't so great and the chances of success (positive messages) are high. Like most of us, Aaron first learned to drive in a parking lot. A big parking lot. A big, empty parking lot. No matter how much he had studied those books, we would have been lunatics to take him onto the highway during rush hour for his first experience. But he can handle rush hour now. Why? Because he developed some skills in that parking lot, and refined them on the side streets. And these skills became habit patterns; the more he practiced them, the easier driving became, until at some point, he became so accustomed to the driving environment that he doesn't have to think twice about staying on his side of the road in a turn or coming to an easy stop at a red-light.

Habit patterns. That's what happens to technical skills over time, they become ingrained as habits. The more you do something successfully, the easier it becomes to accomplish the next time. From flying an airplane to telling the truth. Or—and this is important—telling a lie. Good habits or bad habits. I mentioned earlier that the

Greek word for habit is *ethiké*. Ethics is all about forming the right kinds of habit patterns. That's the essence of character development. Behaviorally speaking, we are the sum total of our habit patterns; they define us.

The point is simply this: You must follow through with this third step of the process or you will have gotten nowhere.

The question is this: How do we make sure that we are developing the right sorts of patterns, that our actions reflect practical integrity? That is, how can we tell when that sledgehammer is swinging at us, and we're in danger of chunking?

One way is to ask yourself a series of questions. (By the way, these questions are similar to sets of questions developed by many others—Kenneth Blanchard and Norman Vincent Peale, for example, or the famous Four-Way Test of Rotary International.)

1. Is what I'm about to do illegal?

If anything should be a no-brainer, it's this question. Somebody once told me, if you have to ask, you're probably too far down the road already. There is a strong connection between ethics and law and it's right here. The 1991 *Federal Sentencing Guidelines for Organizations* formally established that institutions found culpable for the wrongdoings of their members may have their fines increased by up to 400 percent if they have not created "effective programs to prevent and detect violations of law." On the other hand, if such programs are in place, the *Guidelines* authorize the courts to reduce the fines as well.

It turns out that what the *Guidelines* describe as "effective programs" are ethics programs—exactly the sorts of programs that will create and maintain the right ethical climate in an organization, such as establishing clear standards of conduct, assigning specific individuals responsibility for the programs, and creating methods for communicating standards of behavior, implementing training and monitoring programs, and channels for employees to report problems without fear of retribution.

It turns out that you do the right things for your organization and the law looks more kindly on you if things do go wrong. No surprise there.

But the question of legality isn't enough. So ask a related, but better, question: *Is what I'm about to do apparently illegal?* Much more challenging question. I told you that the only way to influence the ethical climate—the Peer Pressure River—in your organization is by example. Well, here's where it counts. Big time. Ask yourself how your decision will affect the rest of the organization. Will it appear as if you're playing favorites, even if your decision is based on rational, sound thinking? How will it look to your shareholders, or the public? Apply the Mike Wallace Test: Would *60 Minutes* want to make a story out of it? Would you still do what you're about to do if everybody in your neighborhood found out?

You get the idea. This is often a difficult question to answer, simply because we don't know how the public or the employees will react. Yet in most cases, we have a pretty good idea. You may remember the incident in 1994 where Air Force General Joe Ashy was flown from Aviano, Italy, to Colorado Springs aboard a specially equipped VIP C-141 transport aircraft with just himself, his enlisted aide and his pet cat on board. The trip was well within the governing regulations at the time. Yet when *Newsweek* and freelance reporter David Hackworth got hold of that story, it looked like a classic case of government fraud, waste and abuse. So much so that ABC's *20/20* picked up the story and made it sound even sleazier (the enlisted aide was a young female). The point is that the Air Force leadership who authorized the flight—and General Ashy when he arrived at the aircraft—could have foreseen that this was a problem, *even if* no one else found out. This is another example of the chronic disease we talked about at the beginning— *moral myopia.* It's essential that we force ourselves to look at the larger context within which we make decisions. Or else we risk walking into an ethical nightmare.

2. *Is what I'm about to do fair?*

Great question. Often misunderstood. You hear a lot today about fairness, one group or another complaining about unfair treatment. Quite a few times it turns out that those who are complaining don't really understand the term they're using. They use "fair" much like we hear our kids use it: "Hey, that's no fair!" They use fair, but what they really mean is something more like: "Excuse me, but that is personally disadvantageous to me." Of course, our kids don't use those words, but the point is that their complaint is more often a matter of self-interest than justice. Something has happened that doesn't benefit them personally.

Unfortunately (just like Peer Pressure), this isn't limited to kids. Here's a test: Imagine our cashier (remember Mr. Trainee?) in two different scenarios. In the first, he owes you $15 in change but gives you $25. In the second, he owes you $15 but gives you $5. Now I suspect strongly that you would return the extra $10 in the first scenario (especially if you managed to read this far in the book). And you would certainly ask for your $10 in the second. But that's not the point of this mental exercise. What I want you to examine is your emotional reaction to the two situations. Which one gets you more excited, being overcharged or being undercharged? If you're like most of us, it's being overcharged. Think about it: If you are being *under*charged, would the first thought that forms in your mind (even if it doesn't reach your lips) be, "HEY!!

You can't do that to me!"? Probably not. Breaches of fairness seem to be much more powerful when they work against our self-interest. We have to work to get emotionally fired up about breaches of fairness which work for us. (If you don't like the cashier scenario, just think about the last time you saw a referee or umpire make a bad call that helped your team, instead of hurting it.)

The best way to understand fairness in this question is to see it associated with *empathy*. The ability to identify with someone else's situation, feeling, point of view. To see the world from another perspective. Without doubt, this is one of the most powerful concepts in ethics. If ethics is about how we should treat each other and the world around us, empathy has got to be our window into really seeing how we ought to act.

It's my belief that if we could increase the amount of empathy in the world by even the tiniest fraction, this would be a much better place to live. Everything from interpersonal relations to international relations would improve. I imagine it would be very difficult to be a terrorist and have empathy for your victims. Similarly, cutting off another driver on the freeway would be a challenge if you had enough empathy for him or her And it would be equally tough to cheat on your taxes if you empathized with the first-grader on the school lunch program who is fed with those taxes.

So the question of fairness is really one of empathy. Ask yourself, "Could I accept the results of my action if I were on the receiving end?" Not, "Would I like it?" since that brings us back to self-interest. Rather, turn the tables and see what it feels like on the other side. That's what I mean by, "Is it fair?"

3.   Am I violating my organizational core values?

Now it's time to put all that quiet thinking you did up in the first step into practice. Examine the choice you're about to make through the filter of your organizational values.   The values are the *ethical* bottom line, the fundamental reasons behind your decisions and actions. Use them to find the right choices.

Be warned that this is a little tougher than you might think. The real danger in answering this question is the *risk of rationalizing.* I have no idea where this fits into Darwin's theory of natural selection, but somewhere along the evolutionary path we as a species developed the fine art of rationalizing, of making up excuses for our actions instead of coming up with good reasons. And we tell these stories not just to those around us, but to ourselves.

That's dangerous. Especially if we really believe what we're saying.

Fortunately, the natural selection process left us with one defense mechanism: That ethics spot. Right in the pit of our stomachs. It's the spot that warns us when we're rationalizing by sending out a pain reminder. Ignore it, and it might go away. Pay attention, and it will alert you to examine carefully the choice you face. It will keep you honest with yourself about the value of your decision.

A Simple Test

If you would like an even simpler version of these questions, here it is, reduced to one simple test: *The Mommy Test.* When you are faced with a choice, when

you're about to act, just ask yourself this one small
question:

> *Would my Mother like me to do this?*

I can just about guarantee that, unless you came from a
very, very dysfunctional family, ninety-nine times out of a
hundred this will prevent you from chunking.

And if by chance you did come from one of those
families, just find someone in your life whom you respect,
look up to. See, it's all about role modeling. As a leader,
you are a role model. And you got that way by watching
your role models. Search your memory, and find the best
model you can. Then put him or her in that approval spot.

This little test is the best single protection there is for your
character. It will shield you from that sledgehammer,
especially in the little decisions. Try it with the small
ones. You'll find that it's quite easy to use. And if you
get good with those, the bigger ones will be easier to

tackle, because you'll be developing the right ethical habits.

The more you keep from chunking, the better those around you will get as well. And the River will flow in the right direction.

Because you will be *hammer-proof.*

FiNAl ThoughTs

There is a lot of material to chew on here, not exactly mental fast food. The question is, did we reach the goal? The goal was to convince you that ethics and values-based thinking do make a difference, and furthermore, that you, as a leader in your organization, are the key to that difference.

Ethics does have an effect on the bottom line, but not necessarily the short-term bottom line. We are looking more at long-term results, but you know as well as I (and probably better than Wall Street speculators) that those are the ones that really count.

Values-based leadership makes a long-term positive difference because it has a powerful cascading effect: It results in increased trust between management and employees, between employees and customers, in fact among all the stakeholders. And increased trust leads to more genuine communication, and that type of communication increases your effectiveness, no matter what business you're in.

Ethical thinking does have its rewards.

When you think about the rewards of developmental leadership, I want you to think about Interface, Inc., an international carpet manufacturer based in Atlanta, Georgia. Interface has the great fortune to be run by two of the finest values-based leaders in any industry, Ray Anderson (Chairman and CEO) and Charlie Eitel (President and Chief Operating Officer). Ray has launched a massive (and to this point highly successful) campaign to convert Interface into a sustainable company, one that takes nothing more out of our earth than it returns; he eventually wants to become restorable—to create a positive ecological "cash flow" with God's capital. How does he see the mixture of ethics and business? "Let's do well by doing good." You can be both profitable and a good steward to the people and planet God has given us. Ray is proving that every day.

From his earliest days as a leader, Charlie Eitel recognized the importance of long-term results in a business strategy. He works to build lasting relationships with his employees, treating them (as he says in his inspiring book, *Eitel Time: Turnaround Secrets*) as his first customers, knowing that they will treat the paying clients exactly as they have been treated. As president of another carpet company before coming to Interface, Charlie began a General Equivalency Diploma (GED) program for his employees on the shop floor who wanted to finish high school. Many companies encourage their employees to continue their education, but Charlie did it differently. He paid his employees to attend classes on company time, four hours a week. He paid for the teachers and tutors. What did he ask for as payback?

Nothing.

Both the *Wall Street Journal* and *NBC Nightly News* got wind of this and came down to look at the program and interview Charlie. They wanted to know if he was worried that an employee would get the diploma and then simply quit. Charlie's response sums up the entire focus of *Hammer-Proof*:

"My job is to create an environment where people will want to stay. If at some point, they want to grow further and our company can't provide new opportunities, so be it; everyone still wins."

Everyone still wins. That's what making a difference is all about. That's why you're in business.

The ethical climate that you are creating is not static; it's a process, a constantly changing process. It requires constant care and attention. If you think things are absolutely great in your organization, look out— complacency will kill you. "Nothing fails like success" (another of Ray Anderson's favorite sayings).

Your job, on a daily basis, is to design an organization in which it is easier, not harder, to do the right thing. You have the power to change the flow of that River, to make Peer Pressure work for you.

Perhaps this is too idealistic, but perhaps not. Look at the power of one person: Mother Theresa. Throughout her life, she believed that we cannot do great things; we can only do small things—greatly.

One final story. This one's well known, but I heard it one night over dinner from a former student and now a good friend of mine, Michael Benson:

A man was walking along an isolated beach after a storm. The waves were still crashing intensely on the shore when he came around a shallow bend. There in front of him, he saw thousands upon thousands of starfish, all washed ashore as a result of the storm, all slowly suffocating. As he walked closer, he saw in the midst of the pile of starfish a small boy, perhaps 6 or 7 years old. As he watched, the boy bent down, picked up a starfish, paused to look at it for a second, and then turned and tossed it back into the water. Then he started again, bending down, picking up a starfish, examining it, tossing it in the water. The man looked at the thousands of starfish and the boy, and saw the utter futility of what this boy was trying to do. Overwhelmed with frustration, he waded through the starfish, came up to the boy and, over the crash of the waves, shouted to him, "STOP IT! You're not making any difference!" The boy stopped for a moment, a starfish in his hand, looked up into the man's eyes and replied, "I am to this starfish," and tossed it into the sea.

Creating and maintaining a positive ethical climate is not easy work, nor is it ever finished. But you can make a difference in that climate. Every day. Leadership carries with it many burdens. But it also carries the potential for great rewards.

What do you want your colleagues to say of you when you're gone? Genuine leaders, I think, can understand how Lao Tse described them in 550 BC when he wrote verse 17 of the *Tao te Ching*:

As a leader, you are best when people barely know you exist,
Not so good when they obey and acclaim you,
Worst when they despise you.
If you fail to honor people, they will fail to honor you;
But if you are a good leader, who talks little,
When your work is done, your aim fulfilled,
They will all say:
'We did this ourselves.'

And so we did.

If you would like to order additional copies of **Hammer-Proof**, please fill out the form below:

Please send me _____ copies of **Hammer-Proof**. I am enclosing $15.95 for each copy ordered, plus $4.00 shipping and handling.

NAME

STREET ADDRESS

CITY   STATE

Mail to:

Jeffrey A. Zink, Ph.D.

Ethics and Leadership Enrichment

2515 Wimbleton Court
Colorado Springs, CO 80920

If you would like to order additional copies of **HAMMER-PROOF**, please fill out the form below:

Please send me _____ copies of **HAMMER-PROOF**. I am enclosing $15.95 for each copy ordered, plus $4.00 shipping and handling.

_____
NAME

_____
STREET ADDRESS

_____
CITY   STATE

Mail to:

Jeffrey A. Zink, Ph.D.

Ethics and Leadership Enrichment

2515 Wimbleton Court
Colorado Springs, CO 80920

If you would like to order additional copies of **Hammer-Proof**, please fill out the form below:

Please send me _____ copies of **Hammer-Proof**. I am enclosing $15.95 for each copy ordered, plus $4.00 shipping and handling.

NAME

STREET ADDRESS

CITY   STATE

Mail to:

Jeffrey A. Zink, Ph.D.

Ethics and Leadership Enrichment

2515 Wimbleton Court
Colorado Springs, CO 80920